Crazy Knitting

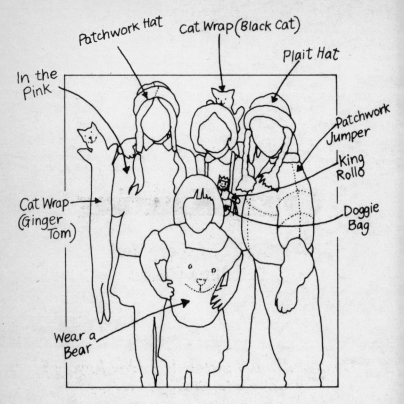

Key to front cover photograph

In the Pink

Patchwork Hat

Cat Wrap (Black Cat)

Plait Hat

Patchwork Jumper

King Rollo

Cat Wrap (Ginger Tom)

Doggie Bag

Wear a Bear

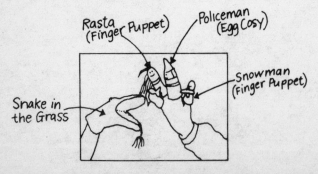

Key to back cover photograph

Rasta (Finger Puppet)

Policeman (Egg Cosy)

Snowman (Finger Puppet)

Snake in the Grass

Crazy Knitting

Sarah Ginsberg and
Caroline Castle

Designed and illustrated by Jane Laycock
Cartoons by Shelagh McGee

Beaver Books

A Beaver Book
Published by Arrow Books Limited
17–21 Conway Street, London W1P 6JD

An imprint of the Hutchinson Publishing Group

London Melbourne Sydney Auckland Johannesburg
and agencies throughout the world

First published 1986

Set in Linoterm Times
by JH Graphics Limited, Reading

Made and printed in Great Britain
by The Guernsey Press Co Ltd,
Guernsey, C.I.

ISBN 941890 8

Contents

(Dots denote difficulty of patterns: ● easy; ●● slightly harder; ●●● you'll probably need a grown-up's help)

Introduction

Be careful! Knitting is such fun that once you've learned you may never stop.

In this book you'll find all the information you need to learn the basic techniques – but even though we've done our best to make things as clear as possible, it's probably still a good idea to find a grown-up to help you start.

There are all sorts of entertaining things to make – for yourself, or for your family and friends. The dots at the top of the page show whether a pattern is easy to make: one dot means it's very easy; two mean medium; three for when you feel a bit more confident.

Happy knitting!

Learning to Knit

Tools and Materials

You only need two things to start knitting – a pair of knitting needles and some yarn.

Needles

Needles are sold in pairs. They're usually made of aluminium, which is light and easy to use. You can also buy plastic and wooden ones. Needles are made in a range of different widths. If you're using thick yarn you'll need big needles. Thinner yarns need thinner needles.

Different countries use different ways of numbering the different sizes of needles. Here's a chart for reference.

Needles Conversion Chart

mm	UK	US
2¼	13	0
2¾	12	1
3	11	2
3¼	10	3
3¾	9	4
4	8	5
4½	7	6
5	6	7
5½	5	8

6	4	9
6½	3	10
7	2	10½
7½	1	11
8½	00	13
9	000	15

Keep your needles flat in a box as they can easily get bent. It's difficult to work well with bent needles and impossible to measure your work accurately.

It's also useful to keep quite a different kind of needle to hand when you're knitting: a crochet hook, for picking up dropped stitches (*see p. 54*).

Yarn

You can knit with almost anything – string, cotton, fine ribbon, wool, even thin elastic! So yarn just means knitting thread. The yarn that you buy in shops is made up of single threads twisted together. These threads are called ply. Fine yarns – two or three play – are often used for baby clothes and delicate shawls. Double knitting is made from four ply. Extra thick yarns can be used for making jackets and heavy sweaters.

Today you can buy all kinds of interesting yarns, both natural and man-made. Mohair is fluffy and is the hair of a special kind of goat. Angora is the fur of angora rabbits. These are both very expensive, as are some of the novelty yarns such as poodle and metallic. Wool is probably still the most popular knitting yarn as it's pleasant to work with and wears well.

Yarns are sold by weight, in packs or balls weighing 20, 25, 50 or 100 grams. All yarns are dyed in batches called dye lots. The colour can vary a bit with each dye lot, so make sure you buy enough to finish whatever you're making and that it all comes from the same dye lot. The dye lot numbers are always printed on the band around the yarn.

Here are some more useful tools:

a tape measure

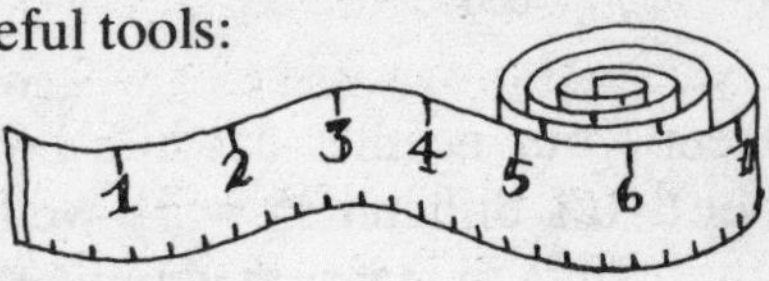

a crochet hook

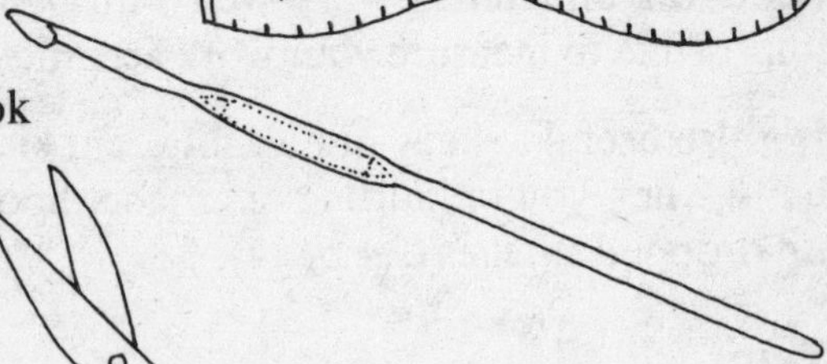

scissors

a blunt needle for sewing up the work

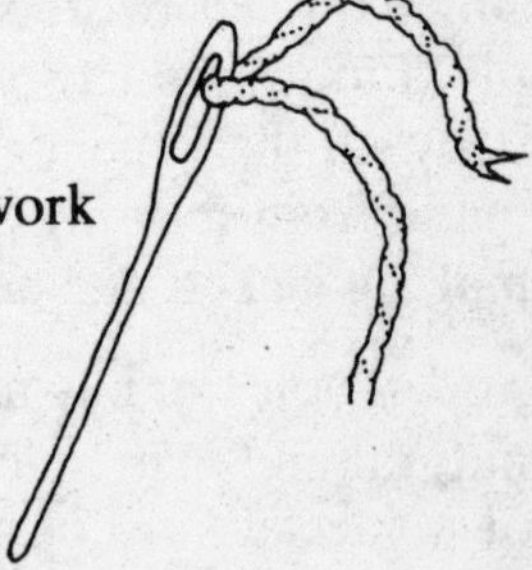

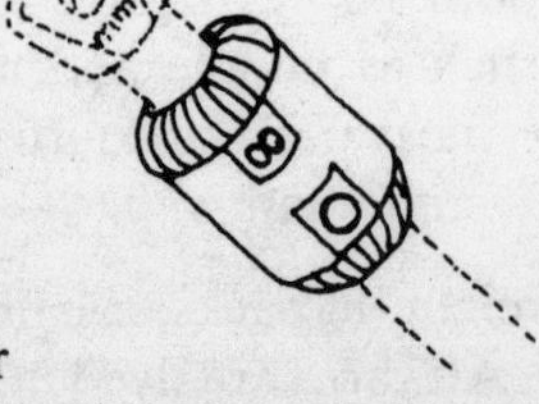

a row counter

Casting On

Sit comfortably when you're knitting. Try not to hunch up your shoulders or you'll find you get tired very quickly, and your knitting will get as tense as you are!

This is the way to hold the yarn.

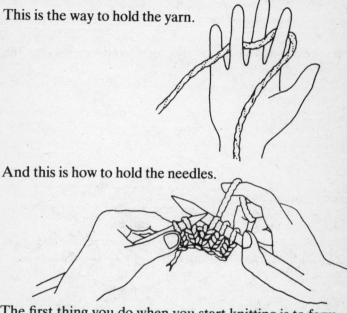

And this is how to hold the needles.

The first thing you do when you start knitting is to form the stitches on the needles. This is called casting on.

1. First make a loop.

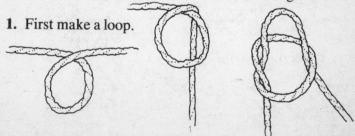

2. Put this on the left-hand needle and pull the yarn tight.

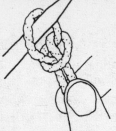

3. Now put the tip of the right-hand needle into the centre of this loop.

4. Wind the yarn around this needle.

5. Draw the yarn through the loop.

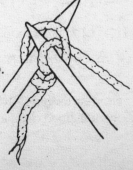

6. Now place the new loop on the left-hand needle.

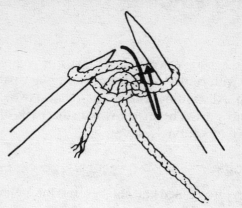

7. For the next stitch, put the right-hand needle *behind* the stitch on the left-hand needle. Pass the yarn around the right-hand needle in the same way as before to make the next stitch. Put this stitch on the left-hand needle.

Continue doing this until you have as many stitches on the left-hand needle as you need.

Knitting Stitches

You can see people wearing all kinds of complicated knitting – with cables on it or bobbles or lacy patterns. Keep calm. All knitting is made up from just two stitches – plain and purl. The magic is that the back of plain knitting is purl knitting!

Plain knitting

This is also often called knit stitches. It is the easier stitch of the two to do. Here's how:

1. Hold the needle with the cast-on stitches in your left hand. Now take the right-hand needle and place the point through the first loop from front to back.

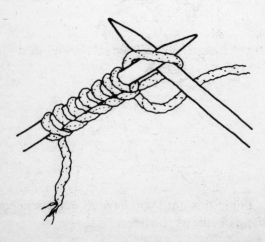

2. Wind the yarn around the tip of the right-hand needle.

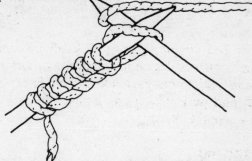

3. Gently pull the yarn through the loop on the left-hand needle.

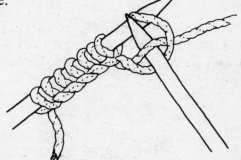

4. Slip the stitch off the left-hand needle, and you've just knitted your first stitch.

Continue in the same way to the end of the row. Then transfer the knitting from your right hand to your left, turning it around so that the back of it is facing you. Now you're ready to begin the next row.

Purl knitting

When you're doing purl stitches, you keep the yarn at the front of the piece of knitting.

1. Place the point of the right-hand needle through the first loop from front to back.

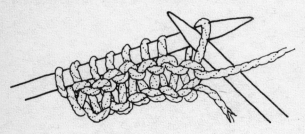

2. Bring the yarn over and round the top of the right-hand needle.

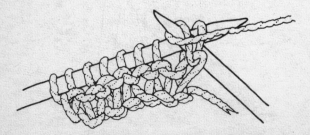

3. Now gently pull the yarn through the loop that's on the left-hand needle.

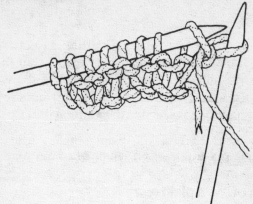

4. Slip the stitch you have just purled off the left-hand needle. Draw the new stitch firmly onto the right-hand needle.

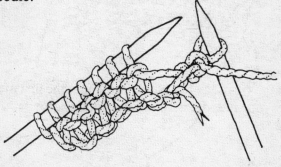

Continue in the same way to the end of the row.

Casting Off

The way to finish off a piece of knitting is to cast off the stitches. You'll need to work very loosely, so that the edge lies flat and does not pucker. One good way to do this is to use a needle (the right-hand one) one size larger than you have been using for the knitting itself.

It looks neat to cast off plain stitches using plain technique, purl using purl. Like this:

Casting off on a plain row

1. Knit two stitches in the usual way.

2. Put the tip of the left-hand needle into the first of the stitches you knitted. Lift this stitch over the second stitch.

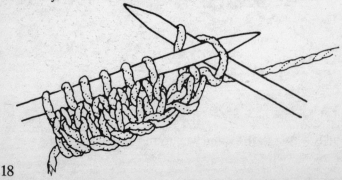

3. Knit the next stitch from the left-hand needle and repeat the process.

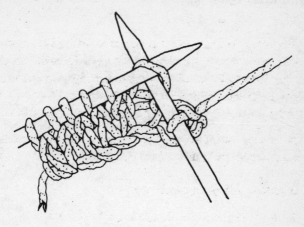

4. When only one stitch is left, break a length of yarn. Draw this through the last stitch and pull it gently and firmly.

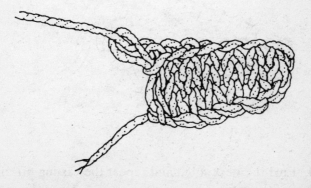

19

Casting off on a purl row

1. Purl two stitches.

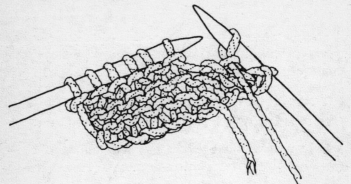

2. Lift the first stitch over the second.

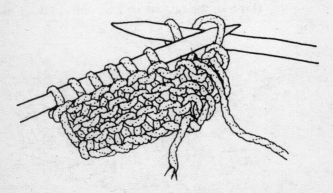

3. Purl the next stitch and repeat the casting off to the end of the row.

Useful Stitches

There's no limit to the ways in which you can combine plain and purl to make amazing patterns and textures. But there are a number of ways in which the stitches are often used.

Garter stitch

This means working every row in plain stitches. It produces a nice ridgy effect and is the easiest way to make a piece of knitting.

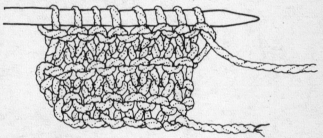

Stocking stitch

This is the pattern that is probably used more often than any other. It is made by knitting one row and purling the next. It's the quickest way to make a piece of knitting grow.

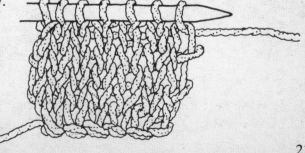

Ribbing

Ribbing is made by knitting one stitch, purling the next, along a row. On the next row you knit the stitches that were purled and purl the plain stitches. You can see what needs doing on the second row in this way. If there's a 'V' on the row below, you need to knit the stitch. If there's a ridge, purl it. Ribbing makes the knitting springy and stretchy, so it is often used for welts (i.e. the bottom edges) and cuffs.

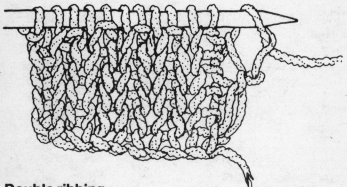

Double ribbing

This makes a firmer texture than single ribbing. It's used in the same way, though, for welts and cuffs. It is made by knitting two stitches, then purling two, to the end of the row. On the next row, purl the knit stitches and knit the purl.

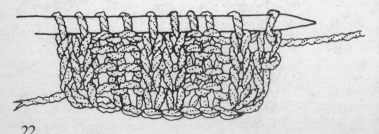

When you are working rib stitches, you will need to change the position of the yarn when you change from plain to purl or from purl to plain.

Changing from plain to purl

Bring the yarn around to the front of the work.

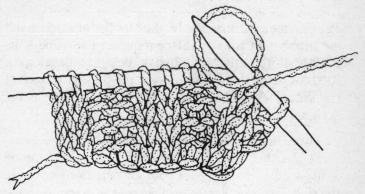

Changing from purl to plain

Put the yarn behind the right-hand needle and then work the stitch.

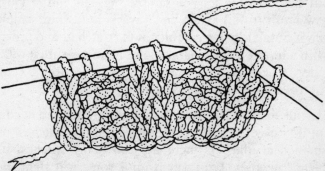

Tension

If you've spent ages making a sweater, it's very disappointing to discover it doesn't fit properly. When this happens it's often because you didn't get the tension right.

Tension means, very simply, the number of stitches and the number of rows to the centimetre. Everyone knits slightly differently, so when a designer develops a pattern, he or she will state what the tension is, so that the knitter can make *exactly* the same garment as the designer.

So at the beginning of every pattern you will find something like this: Tension: 22 sts and 30 rows to 10cm on 4mm needles. In order for your knitting to come out to the right size, you'll need to make sure your tension is the same as that set out in the pattern.

To do this, make a tension sample. Use the yarn, needle size and stitch given in the pattern. Make a square at least 10cm × 10cm. (It's wise to cast on a few more stitches than the tension sample suggests and to knit a few more rows.) When you have knitted your sample, pin it out flat, being careful not to stretch it, and press it with a hot iron and a damp cloth. Now measure it with a ruler. Count how many stitches there are to the centimetre, and how many rows.

If your tension is wrong, try out different sized needles until you get it right. If there are too few stitches, use smaller needles. If there are too many stitches, use bigger needles. Experiment until you get it right. For

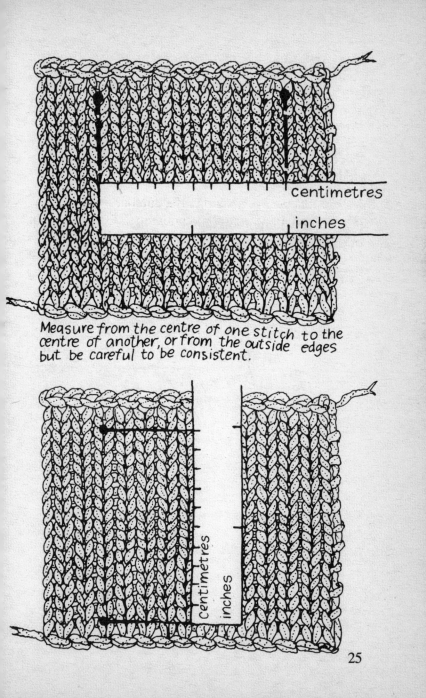

Measure from the centre of one stitch to the centre of another, or from the outside edges but be careful to be consistent.

plain patterns, it's more important to get the right number of stitches to the centimetre. You can always knit a few more or less rows, but if the number of stitches is incorrect you will end up with a garment the wrong size.

All this can seem like a lot of trouble when you're longing to get started but it really is worth it!

P.S. Keep your tension samples. When you've got a pile of them you can make a patchwork blanket.

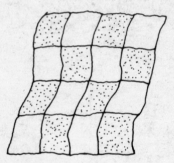

Increasing and Decreasing

In order to give a piece of knitting some shape, you will need to know how to add stitches (increase) and how to lose stitches (decrease). There's a way to do this so that you don't leave any gaps or holes in your knitting.

Increasing
On a knit row

1. Knit into the front of the first stitch in the usual way but don't slip it off the needle.

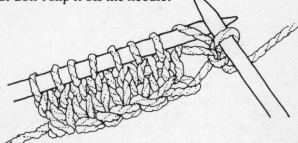

2. Knit again into the back of the same stitch, from right to left.

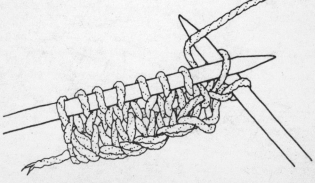

You have now made two stitches out of one.

When you are increasing at the end of a row, it is neater to make the double stitch out of the stitch before the last one.

On a purl row

The technique is exactly the same.

1. Purl into the front of the stitch, but don't drop it off the needle.

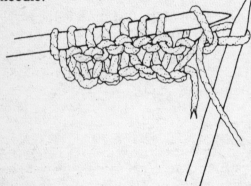

2. Purl again into the back of the same stitch.

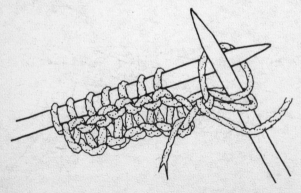

3. This is what the increased stitch looks like.

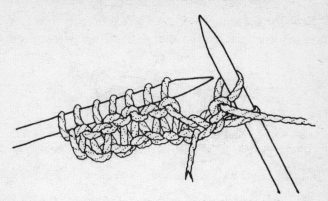

There are other ways of increasing, which are designed to give a pretty effect. You'll sometimes find these in patterns. Here is an example.

Yarn over
On a knit row

1. When you are doing plain knitting the yarn is kept behind the knitting. In the place where you want to make an extra stitch, bring it forward, in front of the knitting.

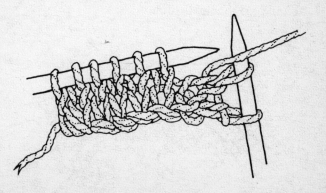

2. Then bring it round to knit the next stitch in the usual way.

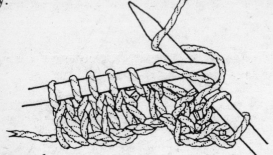

On a purl row

1. On purl rows the yarn is kept at the front of the needle all the time. So to make an extra stitch, you need to wind the yarn right around the needle.

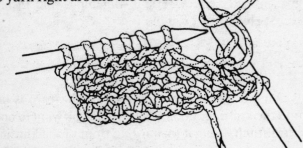

2. Then purl the next stitch.

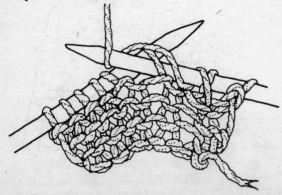

Decreasing

The easiest way to do this is by working two stitches together.

1. Put the needle through the front loop of the first two stitches. Then knit in the usual way.

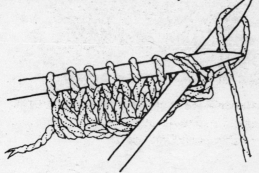

2. On a purl row, put the needle through the first two stitches from the front to the back. Then purl in the usual way.

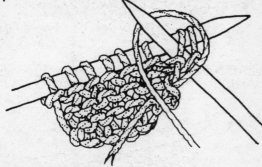

Pass Slipped Stitch Over

This is a way of decreasing which makes a small hole. It is often used in patterns to create a lacy look.

1. Insert the tip of the right-hand needle into the first stitch on the left-hand needle. Do not knit it – just slip it on to the right-hand needle.

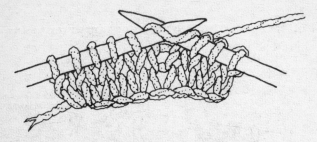

2. Knit the next stitch in the usual way.

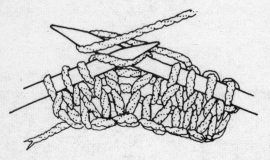

3. Put the point of the left-hand needle through the slipped stitch and lift it over the stitch you have just knitted.

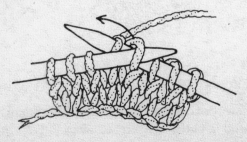

Stripes and Patchwork

Stripes

When you are knitting horizontal stripes you join in the new colour at the beginning of a row.

1. Wind the colour you have been using around the needle. Then loop the new colour over the needle. Knit the stitch with both colours.

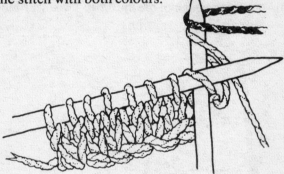

2. Knit the next stitch using both colours as well.

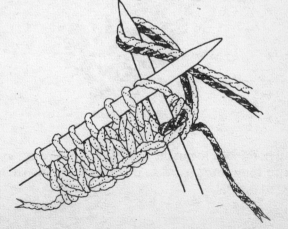

Continue knitting using the new colour by itself. Break off the old colour leaving a length of yarn. On the next row, remember to work the two-colour stitches as if they were each one stitch.

If you are using two colours to make thin stripes you don't need to keep breaking off the yarn when you join in the next colour. If you always join in the second colour after an even number of rows, you can keep the second ball of yarn at the back of the work.

When you want to join in the second colour, strand it loosely up across the back of the knitting. Twist it around the first colour and begin knitting.

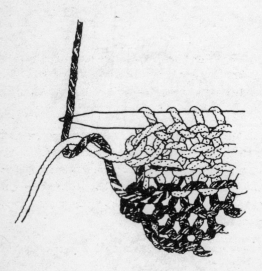

It's a good idea to pin the ball of yarn you're not using to the knitting at the back, so that the two colours don't get twisted together.

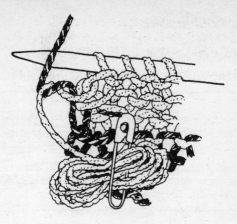

Patchwork

The easiest way to make patchwork is to knit a number of squares the same size and then sew them together. But you'll get a much smoother finish if you knit them as you go.

To do this you will need a separate ball of wool for each square. First of all, find out how much yarn you will need for each square. To do this, use the needles and wool specified and knit a sample square. Break off the yarn. Now unravel the knitting and you have the exact length needed for each square.

Use this to measure out a number of lengths for the different squares.

Next, make a number of bobbins, one for each square. You'll need these to keep the different colours separate – otherwise your yarns will get into a terrible muddle. Untangling them could put you off patchwork for ever.

To make bobbins

1. Cut out a shape like this in cardboard.

2. Wind the lengths of yarn around the bobbins.

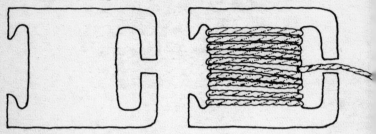

Joining in a new colour

When you need to join in a new colour, the yarns must be loosely twisted together at the back of the knitting to avoid making a hole.

On a knit row

1. Take the bobbin with the new colour in your right hand and take it behind and then over the old colour at the back of the work. The method is the same when you join in a new colour in the middle of a row for the first time.

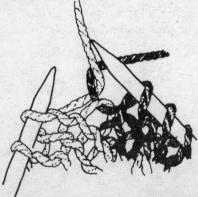

2. Now knit the first stitch of the new colour in the usual way.

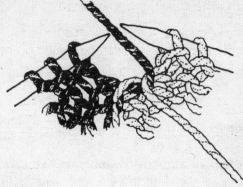

On a purl row

Again, take the bobbin with the new colour over and around the old colour, this time at the front of the work.

Purl the first stitch in the usual way.

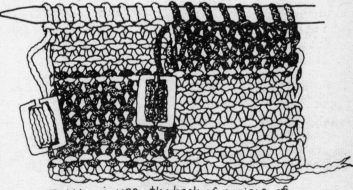

Bobbins in use – the back of a piece of patchwork knitting

37

Decorations

There are all sorts of ways of livening up plain knitting by sewing on decorations.

Fringes

Scarves usually look better with some fringing.

1. Cut lengths of yarn twice the length you want the finished fringe to be. Use three or four lengths for each tassel.

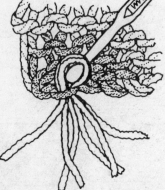

2. Fold them in half. Using a crochet hook, push a hole between the edge of the knitting and the stitches, large enough to push through the lengths of yarn.

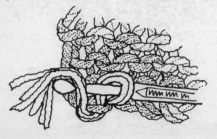

3. Push the crochet hook through the loop and pull through the ends. Tighten them.

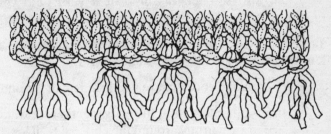

Tassels

These are a simple way to decorate a piece of knitting.

1. Cut pieces of yarn to the length of the finished tassel. Use a crochet hook to draw them under and over a stitch in the knitting.

2. Knot the ends together close to the knitting.

Plaits

You can also sew lengths of plaited yarn onto your knitting.

1. First, decide how long you want the plait to be. Cut lengths of yarn a third longer than this.

2. Tie a knot one end. Plait to within 2.5cm of the end.

3. To finish off, either knot the ends together, or wind a new piece of yarn firmly around the end and tie it.

Pompoms

Nice for hats or to sew on jumpers . . .

1. You'll need some card or cardboard that's reasonably stiff. Cut two circles to the size of the finished pompom. Then cut out two smaller circles from the middle of each piece.

2. Wind the yarn around the two pieces of cardboard until you can't get any more through the middle using your fingers. Then use a sewing needle.

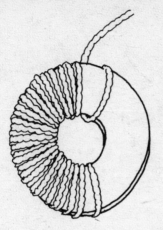

3. With a sharp pair of scissors, cut through all the layers of yarn between the two pieces of cardboard.

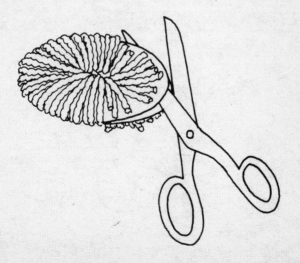

4. Ease the cardboard pieces apart and tie a length of yarn tightly around the middle. Leave a long end free.

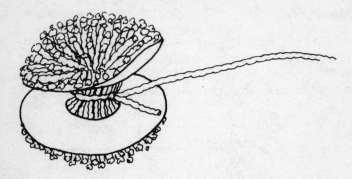

5. Cut or tear off the cardboard and fluff up the pompom. Use the long end to sew it onto your knitting.

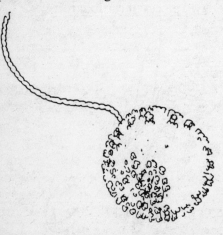

Measuring, Finishing Off and Making Up

Measuring

Always measure your work by putting it on a flat surface. Use a ruler, not a tape measure. Don't stretch the knitting (even if you think it's about time for it to be finished). Make sure the ruler is placed straight, not on a diagonal.

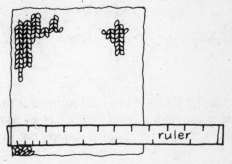

Finishing off

In some ways, how you finish off a piece of knitting is even more important than the knitting itself. Even an uneven piece of work will look terrific if you finish it off carefully.

1. First, sew in the ends. Use a large blunt needle and darn in loose ends across a few stitches. If your knitting is made up of different colours, darn in the ends of each shade on to the same colour.

Before you sew up a garment you need to block and press the pieces.

43

Blocking

. . . means laying each piece out flat on a thick piece of material (an old white sheet, folded up, works well), and pinning it, to check that it is the right shape. Be careful not to stretch it. Use a ruler to check that all the measurements are correct.

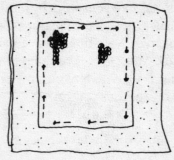

Pressing

Check the instructions on the band around the yarn – some yarns do not need pressing at all. If the yarn can be pressed, leave the pinned-out pieces in position after blocking and lay a damp cloth on top of them. Place a warm iron on top. Don't move it around, just leave it for a few seconds. Then move it to another part of the knitting. Repeat this until it has all been pressed – but don't press any ribbing as this will ruin its stretchiness.

When the knitting is quite dry, unpin it.

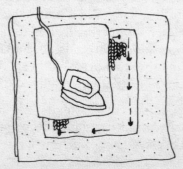

Sewing Up and Looking After Your Knitting

Sewing up

When you are sewing seams together you need to be sure that the two pieces are very evenly placed together. Otherwise one side may become stretched. A good way to do this is to use safety pins at intervals along the seam, unpinning them as you go.

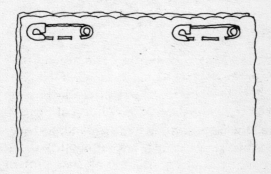

For sewing up a seam, use the same yarn as for the knitting itself unless it is too thick or awkward to use. If it is, find a colour to match it in darning wool or use three or four ply yarn. Use a blunt-ended needle so that you do not split the stitches.

There are different methods of seaming, which suit different parts of a garment. Use back stitch seaming for joining shoulder seams and shaped edges. Use invisible seaming to join stocking stitch or straight edges.

Back stitch seam

1. Put the right sides of the work together. Make a small knot at the end of the length of yarn and draw it through the right-hand edge of the work.

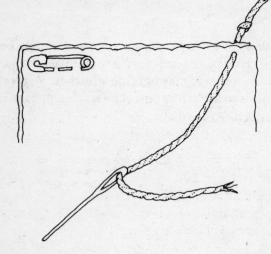

2. Take the needle through the work to the back. Move it across two stitches and bring it through to the front.

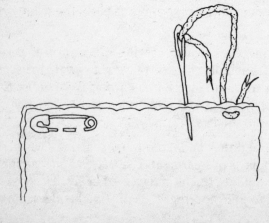

3. Bring the yarn back across one stitch, and push the needle through to the back again.

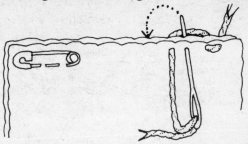

Repeat to the end of the seam. Then darn in the end of the yarn before cutting it off close to the knitting.

Invisible seam

With this method, you keep the right side of the work facing you all the time, so you can see exactly what the finished seam will look like.

1. Put the edges of the work together and pin along the length of the seam as described above. Make a knot in the yarn and make sure this knot is on the wrong side when you draw the yarn through to begin the seam.

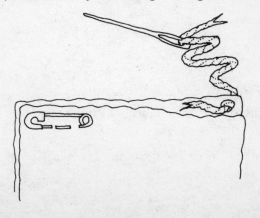

2. Pass the needle between the first two stitches on one of the pieces of knitting.

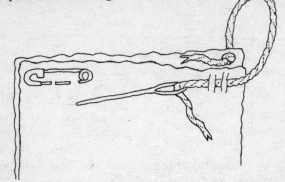

3. Then pass the needle over to the other side of the work and pick up a thread there.

4. Pull the two pieces together gently. Then move the needle across to the first piece of knitting and pick up the next thread.

Continue to the end of the seam. Darn in a length of the sewing yarn before cutting it.

Looking after your knitting

Check the band around the knitting yarn to see if there are any special washing instructions. Wash your knitwear by hand, and use mild soap and warm, not hot, water. Don't soak it, just squeeze it gently, being careful not to pull it out of shape. Rinse several times to get rid of all the soap, or the yarn will spoil.

Then squeeze out as much water as you can, without wringing it, and roll it up in a towel – make sure the towel colour will not run! Leave it for half an hour. Then, when the towel has absorbed as much water as it can, lay the knitting out on another towel, smooth it into shape, and leave it to dry.

Don't hang it on a line or it will stretch out of shape.

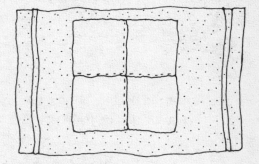

What Have I Done Wrong?

Check your knitting here! These are some common problems and ways to put them right.

How to pick up dropped stitches

On a knit row

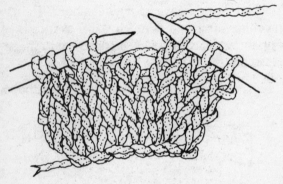

1. Using the right-hand needle, put the tip through the stitch that's dropped and the loop above it.

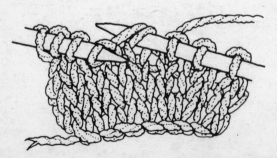

2. Now, use the left-hand needle to lift the stitch on the right needle over the loop.

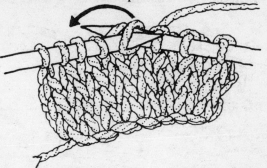

3. Replace the stitch on the left-hand needle, making sure it faces the same way as the other stitches, and continue knitting.

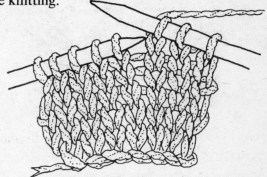

On a purl row

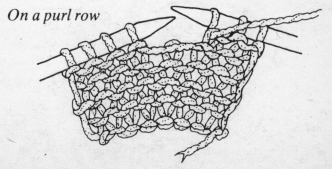

1. Pick up first the dropped stitch and then the strand above it, with the right-hand needle.

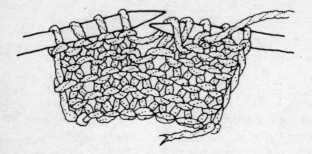

2. Use the tip of the left-hand needle to lift the stitch over the strand.

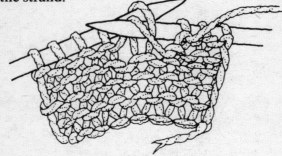

3. Replace it on the left-hand needle.

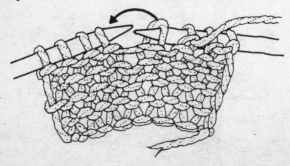

Undoing rows

Sometimes you may need to undo several rows to correct a mistake. The simplest way to do this is to take the knitting off the needle and unravel it until you get to the source of the problem. Unravel the work slowly and carefully, row by row.

To put the stitches back on the needle, hold the knitting in your left hand. Make sure it is turned so that the yarn is at the left-hand edge. Insert the point of the right-hand needle from back to front through each stitch.

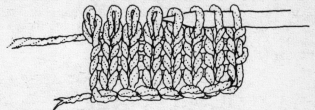

Unpicking mistakes

If you make a mistake either within the row you're knitting or on the row below, you do not need to take the knitting off the needles. You can unpick the stitches one by one until you get to the mistake.

On a knit row

1. Have the knit row facing you. Put the tip of the right-hand needle into the stitch below the one on the left-hand needle.

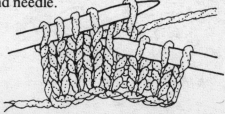

53

2. Slip the stitch off the left-hand needle and gently pull the yarn, which will unravel. Repeat till you get to the mistake.

Use the same method on a purl row, but keep the yarn in front of the work.

Picking up a ladder

If you notice you've dropped a stitch and caused a run, here's what you do. You don't need to unravel a lot of the work. First, be careful not to yank the knitting about, or you'll make the run longer than it is already.

1. Use a crochet hook. Push it through the stitch at the bottom of the ladder, from front to back.

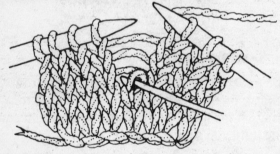

2. Twist the top of the crochet hook around the first 'rung' and draw it through the stitch.

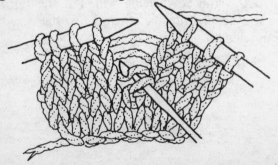

3. Then hook the next rung in the same way and continue until you reach the knitting on the needles. Make sure you put the top stitch back on the left-hand needle facing the same way as the other stitches.

On a purl row – it's more difficult to pick up a ladder on a purl row, so just turn the work around so that the knit side is facing you and pick it up in the same way.

Running out of yarn

It's best to join in a new ball of yarn at the beginning of a row. Do this by placing the new yarn alongside the old and work several stitches using both. Then leave an end of the finished yarn and continue with the new ball. On the next row, be careful to knit the double stitches as one stitch.

If you need to join in a new ball in the middle of a row, the neatest way is by splicing. Unravel the 'plys' in 10cm of the old and 10cm of the new yarn. Cut away half the strands in each. Then twist the old and the new strands together, overlapping a bit at each end. Knit this gently.

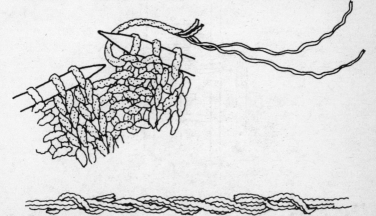

Re-using yarn

If you've got an old jumper than can't be worn any more, or have made a new one that you don't like, don't throw them away. If the yarn isn't too old you can use it again. (Very old yarns tend to lose all their springiness.)

To unravel a jumper, first unpick the seams. There's a special tool you can use to do this, called a seam ripper. Or use a pair of scissors. Then cut through the last stitch of the cast-off edge. Begin unravelling the work. Do it slowly and carefully, as the yarn has a tendency to get caught at the ends of rows.

1. As you work, wind the yarn into hanks around a chair.

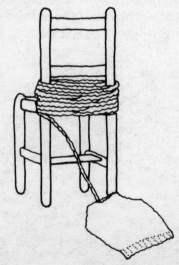

2. As you come to the end of each hank, tie a length of yarn around it.

3. When you've finished, wash the yarn gently in warm soapy water to get all the kinks out. Leave to dry.

4. When the hanks are dry, put each one back over the chair you used originally and re-wind them loosely into balls, ready for re-knitting.

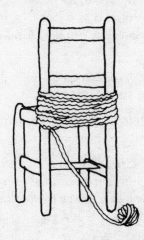

Following a Knitting Pattern

Knitting patterns can look very off-putting to begin with – a muddle of meaningless numbers and letters. They are set out as they are in order to save space. You'll find them easy to follow once you know how.

There are usually three sections to a pattern:

1. At the beginning of a knitting pattern you will find information on the materials you need, the tension, finished sizes and any special abbreviations.

Make sure the pattern is in your size and always buy enough yarn to complete it. If possible, buy the yarn specified in the pattern. If you need or want to use an alternative, remember that you may need more (or less) yarn.

In any case, check your tension and if it's correct, experiment until you get it right (*see page 24*).

2. The second section in a pattern contains the working instructions.

Always read right through a pattern before you begin work. If you think it might be difficult, buy just one ball of yarn and see if you can follow the pattern. Ask someone to explain anything you don't understand.

Follow the instructions in the order they're given. They're set out in the way they are for a reason – for example, a section may need repeating later on, or some parts may need to be sewn together before you can continue.

When you're working keep your place in the pattern with a ruler. Mark the place you've arrived at when you stop working. Try and finish at the end of a row – otherwise you might drop a stitch off the needle or lose your place altogether if it's complicated.

How to read a pattern

Here are all the abbreviations used in this book together with some other ones you may find useful.

Abbreviation	Meaning
alt.	alternate
approx.	approximate
beg.	beginning
cm	centimetre
cont.	continue
dec.	decrease
foll.	following
g.st.	garter stitch
grm	grams
in(s)	inch(es)
inc.	increase
k.	knit
MC	main colour
mm	millimetre
no.	number
p.	purl
patt.	pattern
pr	pair
p.s.s.o.	pass slipped stitch over
rem.	remaining
rep.	repeat
r.s.	right side

sl.1	slip one stitch
st.	stitch
st.st.	stocking stitch
tog.	together
w.s.	wrong side
y.fwd	yarn forward
y.o.	yarn over
y.r.n.	yarn round needle

Here are some other symbols which are also often used.

Asterisks

*k.1, p.1, rep. from * to end of row.

When you see an instruction like that, it means knit one, purl one and repeat this to the end of the row.

Double asterisks

These are used to tell you that you have to repeat a whole section of the pattern. For example:

Work as given for back from ** to **

Look carefully through the instructions for the back and you'll find the section that needs repeating now.

Brackets

There are two kinds of brackets:

1. To indicate different sizes:

Patterns are often set out for different sizes. For example:

To fit 61(66:76:81)cm chest

Later on you will read something like this:

Inc. 3(5:7:7) times more

If you are making the 66cm size then the first instruction after the brackets will be the one you need to follow. Before you start, circle all the instructions for your size. And if there's just one instruction, it means that it is the same for all sizes.

2. A square bracket is sometimes used to show you need to repeat a number of stitches. For example:

[p.1, k.1] 4 times

This means you need to purl one stitch, knit one stitch, four times in all.

The last part of the pattern will give you instructions for sewing it up.

● First-off Scarf

A very easy scarf for your first attempt.

Measurements

20cm × 120cm

You will need

3 50g balls of chunky yarn, 1 pr 6½mm needles and a wool needle for sewing up.

Tension

14 sts = 10cm on 6½mm needles in garter stitch (g.st.).

Instructions

Using 6½mm needles, cast on 23 sts. Work in g.st. until scarf measures 120cm. Cast off.

Making up

Sew in ends of yarn. Make a fringe if you like.

● Handwarming Scarf

A useful extra – sew back the ends
of a scarf to make pockets.

Measurements

25cm × 106cm

You will need

2 50g balls of Jonelle's Softly or other medium weight
fluffy yarn. 1 pr 7mm needles.

Tension

13 sts = 10cm on 7mm needles in garter stitch (g.st.).

Instructions

Leaving a long end of yarn, cast on 25 sts, using 7mm
needles. Work in g.st. until scarf measures 136cm. Cast
off, leaving a long end of yarn.

Making up

To make pockets, fold over 15cm of the scarf at each
end, and sew up the side seams. Sew in loose ends. Fold
pockets inside out.

15cm

● In the Pink!

A stunning pink jumper worked in a lovely soft mohair mixture. It's made up from two basic shapes: 2 squares and 2 oblongs, and knitted on big needles, so it is quick and easy to make, even for a complete beginner. Pockets optional.

Measurements

Chest   75   79   83 cm
Length   44   47   50 cm

For ages 9(11:13)
For the smallest size follow the first number; for the next size, follow the second number, etc.

You will need

8(9:9) 25g balls of Patons Mohair Focus (or equivalent) in shocking pink, 1 pr 5½ mm needles and a wool needle.

Tension

16 sts × 19 rows = 10cm in stocking stitch (st.st.).

Instructions
Front and back (both the same)

Cast on 64(68:72) sts. Work 4 rows in g.st. Cont. in st.st. until work measures 40(43:46) cm. Work in k.1, p.1 rib for 4cm. Cast off loosely.

Sleeves (both the same)

Cast on 49(49:53) sts. Work 4 rows in g.st. Cont. in st.st. until work measures 31(33:35)cm. Cast off loosely.

Pockets (optional): (make 2)

Cast on 20 sts and work in st.st. for 10cm. Work 3 rows g.st. Cast off.

Making up

Block pieces. Do not press. Put front and back pieces right sides together and sew for 10cm along from each shoulder edge, leaving a neck opening. Open out work and lay right side down on flat surface.

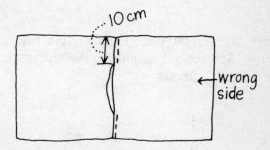

Match centre points of sleeves to shoulder seams. Pin and then sew in.

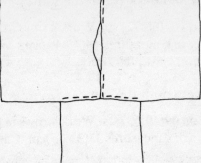

For pockets, turn work right side out. Using backstitch, sew in each pocket at bottom of work, 5cm in from both side seams.

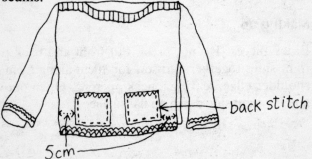

back stitch

5cm

Turn work right sides together; pin side and sleeve seams. Sew seams beginning at the base of work.

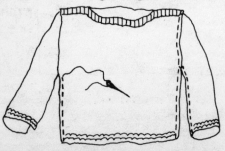

● Easy Street

As long as you can knit in garter stitch you can make this warm, chunky jumper to wear over a shirt or blouse.

Measurements

Chest   67 75 79 83 cm
Length   41 44 47 49 cm

Ages 7(9:11:13)
For the smallest size, follow the first number; for the next size, follow the second number, etc.

You will need

6 balls Patons Beehive Chunky in colour of your choice, 1 pr 6½ mm needles and a wool needle.

Tension

15 sts × 25 rows = 10cm in garter stitch (g.st.).

Instructions
Front and back

Cast on 49(52:55:58) sts and work in g.st. for 41(44: 47:49)cm. Cast off loosely.

Sleeves (make 2)

Cast on 46(49:52:54) sts and work in g.st. for 34(36:38:40)cm. Cast off loosely.

Making up

Do not press. Put front and back pieces together and sew 7(8:9:10)cm along from each shoulder edge, leaving a neck opening. Open out work and lay flat. Match centre of sleeve to shoulder seam. Pin and sew.

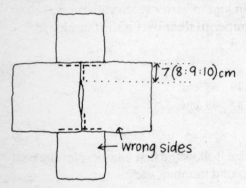

↕ 7(8:9:10)cm

← wrong sides

Pin side and sleeve seams and sew, beginning at bottom edge.

Wear over a shirt or blouse.

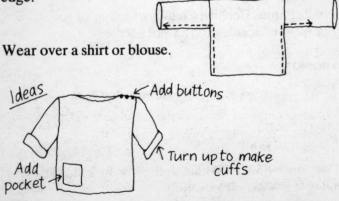

Ideas

↙ Add buttons

Add pocket →

↑ Turn up to make cuffs

●● Stripy Legwarmers

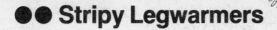

These legwarmers are made out of three different yellows, and three different kinds of ribbing.

Measurements

52cm long

You will need

1 50g ball of double-knitting yarn in three shades of yellow – pale, medium and dark. 1 pr 3¾mm needles, 1 pr 5mm needles and a wool needle.

Tension

32 sts = 10cm in k.1, p.1 rib on 3¾mm needles.

Instructions

Using 3¾mm needles and the darkest yellow, cast on 48 sts. Work in rows of k.1, p.1 rib until work measures 11cm. Change to 5mm needles, and join in the medium yellow. Work in rows of k.2, p.2 rib until whole stocking measures 28cm. Break off yarn and join in the pale yellow. Work in rows of k.3, p.3 rib until work measures 45cm. Change to 3¾mm needles and the darkest yellow.

Work in rows of k.1, p.1 rib until legwarmer measures 52cm. Cast off. Repeat for second leg.

Making up

Sew in loose ends. Sew up seams.

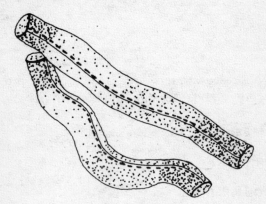

● Sensational Summer Slipover

Measurements

Chest	56	61	66	cm
Length	39	42	45	cm

You will need

1 50g ball of Paton's Cotton Top in pale green and 1 ball in lemon yellow. 1 pr 4mm needles and a wool needle.

Tension

17 sts × 24 rows = 10cm on 4mm needles in stocking stitch (st.st.). For the smallest size, follow the first number. For other sizes, follow the headings for the size you need, e.g. 56(61:66)cm chest.

Instructions
Back and front (both the same)

Using 4mm needles and pale green, cast on 52(58:60) sts. Work in rows of k.1, p.1 rib for 4mm. Break off green yarn and join in yellow. Work in rows of st.st. until work measures 21(23:25)cm. Break off yellow yarn and join in green. Work 4cm of k.1, p.1 rib. Cast off.

Straps (make 2)

Using pale green yarn, cast on 6 sts. Work in rows of k.1, p.1 rib for 28(30:32)cm. Cast off.

Making up

Block pieces. Do not press. Sew up side seams. Sew on
straps, setting them 3cm in from the side seams.

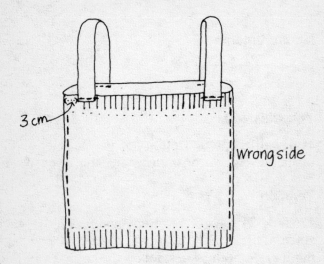

3 cm

Wrong side

●● Simple Ankle Socks

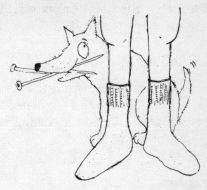

Socks are much easier to make than you might imagine, especially if you use our simple pattern! Here we provide a basic pattern for knitting a plain pair of socks, together with ways the pattern can be adapted by a more experienced knitter.

Measurements

Length 38cm; width, when flat, 20cm
Shoe sizes 3–5

You will need

About 50g double-knitting yarn in colour of your choice, 1 pr 4mm needles, 1pr 4½mm needles and a wool needle.

Abbreviations

sl.1 = slip one stitch
p.s.s.o. = pass slipped stitch over

Tension

20 sts × 26 rows = 10cm in stocking stitch (st.st.) on 4½m needles.

Instructions:

Using 4mm needles, cast on 34 sts and work 12 rows in k.1, p.1 rib. Change to 4½mm needles and cont. in st.st. until work measures 34cm, ending with a p. row.

Shape toe

Next row: *k.1, k.2 tog., k.11, sl.1, k.1, p.s.s.o., k.1. Rep. from * to end.
Next row: p.
Next row: *k.1, k.2 tog., k.9, sl.1, k.1, p.s.s.o., k.1. Rep. from * to end.
Next row: p.
Next row: *k.1, k.2 tog., k.7, sl.1, k.1, p.s.s.o., k.1. Rep. from * to end.
Next row: *p.1, p.2 tog., p.5, p.2 tog., p.1. Rep. from * to end.
Next row: *k.1, k.2 tog., k.3, sl.1, k.1, p.s.s.o., k.1. Rep. from * to end.
Cast off.
Repeat for second sock.

Making up

Lightly press pieces with a cool iron on wrong side. Right sides together, sew back seam.

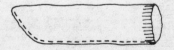

●● Mod Socks

Measurements and tension

As before.

You will need

25g double-knitting wool in both black **A** and white **B**. 1 pr 4mm needles, 1 pr 4½mm needles and a wool needle.

Instructions

Using 4mm needles and **A** cast on 34 sts and work 12 rows in k.1, p.1 rib. Do not break off **A**. Change to 4½mm needles and **B** and work 4 rows in st.st. ending with a p. row. Begin pattern.

How to knit in two colours:

Knit to where you want to change colour. Hold yarn of 1st col. downwards. Then pass 2nd col. across stitches (pull work to full extent or it will pucker) and over yarn of 1st col. and knit as usual.

The back of the work should look like this:

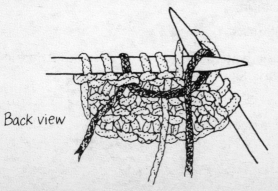

Back view

75

Next row: k.2 in **B**; pick up **A** and k.4; k.3 in **B**; k.6 in **A**; k.4 in **B**; k.4 in **A**; k.3 in **B**; k.5 in **A**; k.3 in **B**.

Work 4 rows st.st. in **B**:

Next row: p.6 in **B**; p.5 in **A**; p.2 in **B**; p.7 in **A**; p.4 in **B**; p.5 in **A**; p.5 in **B**:

Work 4 rows st.st. in **B**.
Repeat the 10 rows of pattern twice more.
Change to **A** and cont. in st.st. until work measures 35cm ending with a p. row.
Shape toe as for basic pattern. Repeat for second sock.

Making up

Darn in loose ends. Press lightly with a damp cloth on wrong side. Sew back seam.

Drawing of back of work showing knitting with 2 colours

For stripy socks

Follow basic pattern, but work in alternate stripes of 2 rows each colour.

Shape toe in one colour.

76

●● Stripy Strip Knit

This sweater is easy to knit
as it is made up entirely from strips
of knitting sewn together.

Measurements

(The figures in brackets state the number of 50g balls you
will need in each colour)

Chest	56 (1)	61 (1)	66 (1)	71 (2)	76 (2)	81 (2)	cm
Length	32	37	41	44	47	49	cm
Sleeve Seam	26	29	32	35	37	37	cm

You will need

50g balls of double-knitting wool in the following colours:
purple **A**   blue **B**   yellow **C**
1 pr 4mm needles, 1 pr 3½mm needles and a wool needle
for sewing up.

Tension

22 sts = 10cm and 32 rows in stocking stitch (st.st.) on
4mm needles. For the smallest size follow the first
number. For the other sizes follow the headings for the
size you need, e.g. 56(61:66:71:76:81)cm chest.

Instructions

Back and front (6 strips)

Using 4mm needles and **A**, cast on 21(23:25:27:28:30) sts. Work in st.st. until knitting measures 26(31:35:38: 41:43)cm. Cast off. Make one more strip in **A**. Then knit two strips in **B** and two in **C**.

Welts (make 2)

Using 3½mm needles and **A**, cast on 63(69:75:81:84:90) sts. Work in rows of k.1, p.1 rib until work measures 6cm. Cast off.

Sleeves (made up of 2 strips each)

Using 4mm needles and **A**, cast on 23(27:29:32:34:35) sts. Work in st.st. until knitting measures 32cm. Cast off. Make one more strip in **A** and two in **C**.

Cuffs (make 2)

Using 3½mm needles and **A**, cast on 46(54:58:64:68:70) sts. Work in k.1, p.1 rib until work measures 6cm. Cast off.

To make up

Block and press all pieces except cuffs and welts. Right sides together, sew one set of three strips together for the front and another for the back.

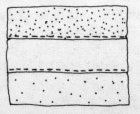

Sew shoulders together by placing the front and back right sides together and sewing 6cm in from the shoulder edge to leave a neck opening. Now sew the strips for the sleeves together and place them so that the join of the two colours is in a straight line with the shoulder seam. Sew the sleeves to the jumper.

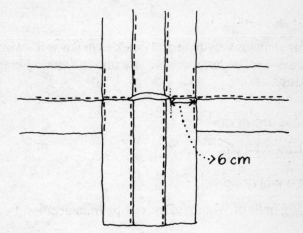

>6 cm

Sew on the welts and the cuffs.

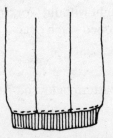

Lastly, sew side seams and sleeve seams.

●●● White Shawl

This shawl is very light and quick to make as it's worked in fine wool on large needles. Be sure to knit very loosely, though.

Measurements

80cm × 140cm

You will need

5 50g balls of Wendy's Dolce, 1 pr 7mm needles.

Abbreviations

y.r.n. = yarn round needle
sl.1 = slip one stitch (pass the next stitch on the left-hand needle onto the right without working it)
p.s.s.o. = pass slipped stitch over

Tension

12 sts = 10cm in pattern below on 7mm needles.

Instructions

Cast on 97 sts. k. 6 rows.
Next row: k.1, *k.3, p.2. Rep. from * to last st, k.1.

Next row: k.1, *k.2, p.3. Rep. from * to last st, k.1.
Next row: k.1, *k.3, p.2. Rep. from * to last st, k.1.
Next row: k.1, *k.2, p.3. Rep. from * to last st, k.1.
Next row: k.1, *y.r.n. to make 1 st., sl.1, k.2 tog., p.s.s.o., y.r.n., p.2. Rep. from * to last st, k.1.
Next row: k.1, *k.2, p.3. Rep. from * to last st, k.1.
These last six rows form the pattern. Repeat them until work measures 137cm, finish the six rows of the pattern, then work six rows in g.st. Cast off.

Making up

Cut strands of yarn 40cm long. Using three strands together, make fringes around three sides of the shawl.

● Pom-Tiddly-Om-Pom!

Here's a really unusual eye-catching scarf that involves no knitting at all – for it's made entirely from pompoms!

Measurements

10cm × 100cm

You will need

2 100g balls of double knitting yarn in contrasting colours (**A** and **B**), (or make up your own colour scheme using oddments), cardboard and a wool needle.

Instructions

Put 2 pieces of cardboard together, one on top of the other. Draw a circle with a 7cm diameter. Cut this out and then draw another circle in the centre with a 1.5cm diameter and cut out.

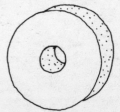

Following the instructions on p. 40, make 20 pompoms in each colour. Trim all loose ends. Thread wool needle with a length of yarn measuring 130cm and tie a large knot in the end. Beginning with colour **A** slip on 20 pompoms in alternate colours and secure end.

Repeat with remaining 20 pompoms, starting with colour **B**. You now have 2 long strings of pompoms.

Making up

Thread your wool needle with a long length of yarn and tie a large knot in the end. Lay the 2 strings of pompoms side by side and thread needle through bottom 2 pompoms. Following diagram, sew the 2 strings of pompoms together. Secure ends.

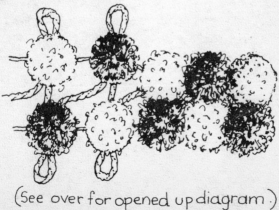

(See over for opened up diagram.)

83

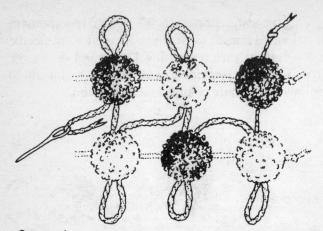

Opened up diagram to show threading sequence

●● Wear a Bear

An unusual, fun jerkin to wear over a skirt or blouse. It's worked on big needles and uses only 2–3 balls of yarn.

Measurements

Chest sizes   63   67   75cm

For ages 5(7:9)

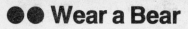

36(38:40)cm

35(37:39)cm

For the smallest size you follow the first number, for the next size you follow the second number, etc.

You will need

2(3:3) 50g balls of Patons Diana Brushed Chunky in Primrose, 1 pr 6mm needles. Scraps of blue, brown and red yarn for embroidering face and a wool needle.

Tension

14 sts × 18 rows = 10cm in stocking stitch (st.st.) on 6mm needles.

Instructions
Front and back (both the same)

*Begin with ears by casting on 12 sts and working 2 rows in st.st.
Next row: Increase 1 st. at beg. and end of this knit row

by knitting twice into first and last st. (*see p. 27*).

Next row: p.

Repeat these 2 rows until you have 18 sts. Work 2 more rows in st.st.

Next row: k.2 tog. Knit to last 2 sts, k.2 tog.

Next row: p.

Repeat these 2 rows until you have 12 sts left.*

At beg. of next row cast on 18(20:22) sts. Do not knit across row, but break off yarn and push first ear and these new sts to end of needle.

Make another ear following instructions above from * to *. Then, right sides facing, slip the 12 sts of new ear on to needle holding other ear.

Knit across all 42(44:46) sts. Cont. in st.st. until work measures 16(18:19)cm ending with a p. row.

Cast on 3 sts at beg. of next 2 rows, 48(50:52) sts. Cont. in st.st. until work measures 27(29:31)cm ending with a p. row.

Next row: k.2 tog. Knit to last 2 sts, k.2 tog. 46(48:50)sts.

Next row: p.

Repeat these 2 rows 3 times: 40(42:44) sts.

Next row: k.2 tog. (twice). Knit to last 4 sts, k.2 tog. (twice) 36(38:40)sts.

Next row: p.2 tog. (twice). Purl to last 4 sts, p.2 tog. (twice).

Cast off remaining 32(34:36)sts.

Making up

Press *very* lightly with a cool iron on wrong side. Embroider face, right side facing.

Right sides together, join shoulder seams.

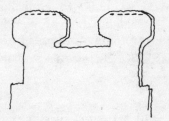

Then right sides together, join side seams.

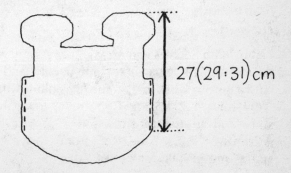

27(29:31)cm

●● Plait Hat

If you're bored with your hairstyle, give yourself a new look with our plait hat – and keep your ears warm at the same time!

For a child of 8 or more.

You will need

Hat: 2 balls of Wendy Chunky (or equivalent) in colour of your choice **A**. Plaits: 1 ball of Wendy Chunky in Seville (yellow) **B**. 1 pr 6mm needles, 1 pr 7mm needles. Piece of cardboard 28 × 20cm and a wool needle.

Tension

13 sts × 17 rows = 10cm in stocking stitch (st.st.) on 7mm needles.

Instructions
Hat

Using 6mm needles and **A** cast on 72 sts and work in k.2, p.2 rib for 8cm. Change to 7mm needles and, beginning with a p. row, work in st.st. for 7cm ending with a p. row.
Next row: *k.2, k.2 tog. Rep. from * to last 4 sts, k.4 (55 sts). Cont. in st.st. for 5 rows.
Next row: *k.2, k.2 tog. Rep. from * to last 3 sts, k.3 (43 sts). Cont. in st.st. for 3 rows.

Next row: k.2 tog. to last st., k.1 (21 sts).
Next row: p.
Next row: k.2 tog. to last st., k.1 (11 sts).
Next row: p.
Next row: k.2 tog. to last st., k.1 (6 sts).
Break off yarn, thread through remaining 6 sts and secure.

Making up

Darn in loose ends. Avoiding ribbing, press work on wrong side with a damp cloth. Turn hat inside out and sew back seam.

Plaits

Cut out a piece of cardboard 38 × 20cm. Using **B** wind yarn round cardboard lengthwise to make a skein.

Then cut across both ends.

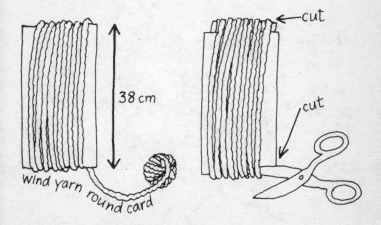

You now have 2 equal lengths of yarn for plaiting.

Tightly tie tops of plaits with a piece of yarn.

Tie tightly   Tie tightly

Divide into three equal sections and plait. Secure ends with a short length of yarn. Trim ends level.

Making up

With hat turned wrong side out and seam at back, stitch in plaits, overlapping ends by 1cm from top of ribbing.

Turn hat right side out and turn up 4cm of rib to make brim. You could decorate the hat with a pompom and add bows to the plaits.

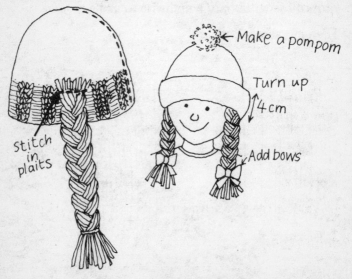

Stitch in plaits

Make a pompom

Turn up
4cm

Add bows

You are now ready to amaze your family and friends with your new hair style!

●●● Cat Wrap

A cheerful cat that is both a warm, snuggly scarf *and* a puppet! Make a Ginger Tom with orange and cream stripes, or a lucky black cat. This pattern is for more experienced knitters, or for beginners to make with help.

Measurements

Length: 120cm

You will need

2 100g balls of brushed chunky in black; or 1 in orange and 1 in cream for the Ginger Tom. 1 pr 5mm needles. Small quantities of red, blue and brown for embroidering face and a wool needle.

Tension

18 sts × 20 rows = 10cm in stocking stitch (st.st.).

Instructions

Note: For Ginger Tom, begin legs with 4 rows cream, then work in stripes of two rows cream and two rows orange.

Left leg

With 5mm needles cast on 16 sts and work in st.st. for 17cm, ending with a p. row. At beg. of next row, cast on 4 sts. Do not knit across row, but break off yarn and push work to end of needle.

Right leg

Cast on 16 sts and work in st.st. for 17cm ending with a p. row. Slip right leg on to needle holding left leg. (You may have finished like this anyway.)

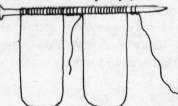

At beg. of next row, cast on 2 sts then knit across all 38 sts. At beg. of next row, cast on 2 sts and p. across all 40 sts. Cont. in st.st. until work measures 103cm, ending with a p. row.

Make arm holes

Next row: k.10, turn. Cont. on these 10 sts for another 8 rows. Break off yarn. Join yarn at remaining sts, k.20, turn. Cont. on these 20 sts for another 8 rows. Break off yarn. Join yarn at final 10 sts, k.10, turn. Cont. on these 10 sts for 8 rows.

Turn and p. across all 40 sts.

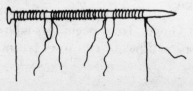

Work 2 rows in st.st.

Shape neck

Next row: *k.4, k.2 tog., k.4. Rep. from * to end (34 sts).
Next row: p.
Next row: k.3, k.2 tog. Continue knitting 2 tog. to last 3 sts, k.3 (20 sts).
Next row: p.
Cast off loosely.

Arms (make 2)

For Ginger Tom, beg. with 4 rows cream, then cont. in stripes of 2 rows each col.

Cast on 12 sts. Work 8cm in st.st. ending with a p. row. Cast off.

Face (make 2)

Cast on 10 sts.
First row: increase 1 st. at beg. and end of row by knitting twice into first and last st. (*see p. 27*).
Next row: p.
Rep. these 2 rows twice more (16 sts). Cont. on these 16 sts until work measures 7cm, ending with a p. row.
Next row: k.2 tog. Knit to last 2 sts, k.2. tog.
Next row: p.
Rep. these 2 rows twice more (10 sts). Cast off loosely.

Ears (make 4)

(*Note:* For Ginger Tom, work in cream only.)
Cast on 6 sts, p.1 row.
Next row: k.2 tog. Knit to last 2 sts, k.2 tog.

Next row: p.
Next row: k.2 tog., k.2 tog.
Next row: p.
Next row: k.2 tog. and thread yarn through remaining st. and secure.
Repeat three times so you finish with 4 pieces.

Tail

Cast on 12 sts and work in st.st. for 15cm. Cast off. For Ginger Tom, beg. with 4 rows cream.

Making up

Block out pieces and press *very* lightly on wrong side with a damp cloth.

Body

Lay work flat with right side facing; turn over two sides so centre seam is in middle of back.

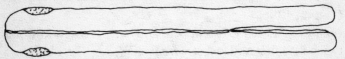

Legs

Pin leg seams and sew. Sew 3cm down back seam from neck, then leave a gap of 12cm before continuing back seam to bottom of piece.

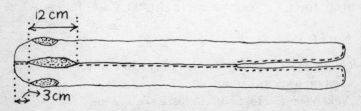

Arms

Turn right sides together and sew arm seams leaving top end open.

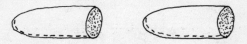

Then embroider face:

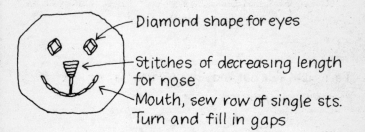

Diamond shape for eyes

Stitches of decreasing length for nose

Mouth, sew row of single sts. Turn and fill in gaps

Then, right sides together, sew head seam leaving gap at neck:

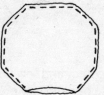

Ears

Wrong sides together sew two ear pieces together:

Repeat for second ear.

Sew arms to body with arm seams facing downwards (see diagram). Pin head in place and sew:

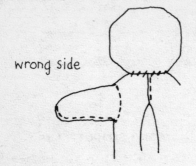

Turn right side out and sew on ears:

Tail

Turn right sides together and sew tail seam leaving gap at end. Turn right side out and sew on to back:

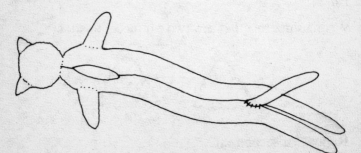

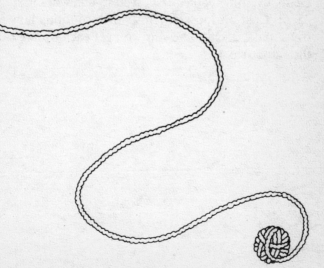

All Square

Everything in this section is made from squares. So if you can knit in stocking stitch, you can make any of the garments here. You don't even have to know how to increase or decrease – it couldn't be simpler!

First, we will tell you how to make your squares, then it's up to you to choose what to make. The variations of colour and style are endless.

● Basic Square Pattern

You will need

25g balls of Paton's Mohair Focus (2 balls make 3 squares) or equivalent. 1 pair 6½mm needles and a wool needle.

Tension

12 sts × 17 rows = 10cm in stocking stitch (st.st.) on 6½mm needles.

Measurements

Each square 25 × 25cm

Instructions

Using 6½mm needles cast on 30 sts and work in st.st. for 25cm. Cast off loosely. (It is worth counting how many rows make 25cm to be sure you get each square exactly the same size.)

● Patchwork Jumper

Measurements

48 × 48cm (when sewn)
Chest   75   79   83 cm
For a child of 10 or more

You will need

8 balls of Patons Mohair Focus as follows: 2 in red, 2 in blue, 2 in green and 2 in black. If you prefer, you could make up your own colour scheme.

Instructions
Body

Make 2 squares in each colour.

Sleeves

Make four squares as follows:
1 and 2: work 12.5cm in black and 12.5cm in green.

```
Green

Black
```

3 and 4: work 12.5cm in blue and 12.5cm in red.

```
Blue

Red
```

Making up

Do not press.

Front

Sew 2 body squares right sides together as follows:

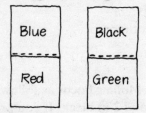

You now have a left and right side.

Pin the two sides right sides together, making sure all squares join neatly at centre. Sew centre seam.

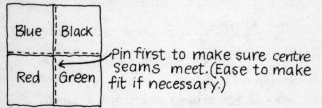

Diagram shows work opened out.

Back

Make up as for front, but arrange squares like this:

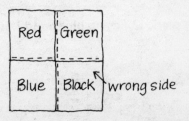

Sleeves (both the same)

Put right sides together and pin sleeve seams making sure all colours meet at the same point. Colours should be arranged as follows:

Sew top sleeve seam.

Black	Blue
Green	Red

Both sleeves are like this.

Neck

Arrange work as follows, and sew 9cm along from shoulder edge on each side.

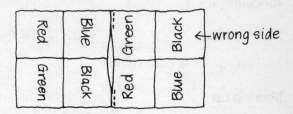

Red	Blue	Green	Black
Green	Black	Red	Blue

←wrong side

Finally, lay work flat and match sleeve seams to shoulder seams as follows.

Pin and sew.

	Black	Blue	
	Green	Red	
Red	Blue	Green	Black
Green	Black	Red	Blue
	Red	Green	
	Blue	Black	

←wrong side

Pin and sew side seams, beginning at bottom edge.

You can, of course, wear your jumper either way round!

● Easy Patchwork Hat

You will need

2 balls of Patons Mohair Focus in contrasting colours. (For the hat on the front cover, we used black and shocking pink.)

Instructions

Make 1 square in each colour.

Making up

Wrong sides together, sew two side seams for 8cm.

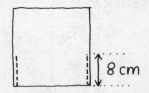

Turn so right sides are together and finish seam.

Gather top, pull tight and secure.

You will be left with a small gap. Turn work wrong side out and sew.

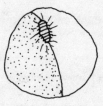

Turn right side out and turn up 8cm to make brim.

Make a pompom with the left-over yarn.

●Matching Scarf

You will need

4 balls of Paton Mohair Focus as follows: 2 in black and 2 in pink.

Instructions

Make 3 squares in each colour. Sew together as follows:

Black	Pink	Black	Pink	Black	Pink

More ideas for patchwork squares

Add pockets.

Make your squares in stripes of 2 rows of alternate colours.

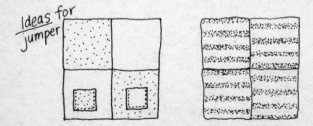

Ideas for jumper

Scrap Book

Never throw away odd scraps of yarn. There's always something you can make, whether it's a finger puppet that uses only a few metres, or a ragbag jumper made up from different types of yarn.

In this section you will find lots of ideas for using up scraps – but be inventive, knitting is a marvellous way to be creative and anyone can make their own designs with a bit of experimenting. Using oddments, it doesn't cost you a thing, either!

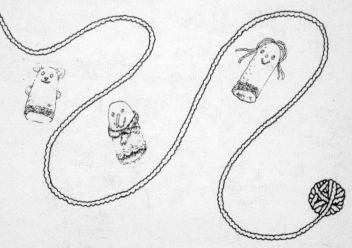

●● Finger Puppets

Finger puppets make lovely presents and they are really easy and quick to make. Here we give basic patterns for the different kinds of yarn you will find in your scrap bag, together with some ideas for characters. But do make up your own – you'll be surprised how easy it is!

Using 4 ply

With 3mm needles cast on 14 sts and work 2 rows in k.1, p.1 rib.
Cont. in st.st. for 14 rows ending with a p. row.
Next row: *k.2, k.2 tog. Rep. from * to last 2 sts, k.2 (11 sts).
Next row: p.
Next row: K2 tog. to last st., k.1 (6 sts).
Thread yarn through remaining 6 sts, gather up and secure. Embroider face, add buttons, etc., when work still flat. Join back seam.

Ideas

Ted
Embroider loops for ears
Make in brown

Girl
Add hair
Make in pink

Clown
Embroider hair
Buttons for eyes
Knit stripes of two rows

Using double knitting

With 4mm needles cast on 12 sts and work 2 rows in k.1, p.1 rib. Cont. in st.st. for 8 rows ending with a p. row.
Next row: *k.2, k.2 tog. Rep. from * to end (9 sts).
Next row: p.
Next row: k.2 tog. to last st., k.1 (5 sts).

Thread yarn through remaining 5 sts, gather up and secure. Embroider face and sew back seam.

A fun idea!

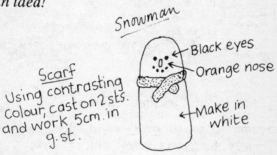

Snowman

Scarf
Using contrasting colour, cast on 2 sts. and work 5cm. in g.st.

Black eyes

Orange nose

Make in white

Using mohair

With 4½mm needles cast on 10 sts and work 2 rows in k.1, p.1 rib. Cont. in st.st. for 6 rows, ending with a p. row.
Next row: *k.2, k.2 tog. Rep. from * to last 2 sts, k.2 (8 sts).
Next row: p.
Next row: k.2 tog. to end of row (4 sts).

Thread yarn through remaining 4 sts, gather up and secure. Finish off as above.

Funky ideas

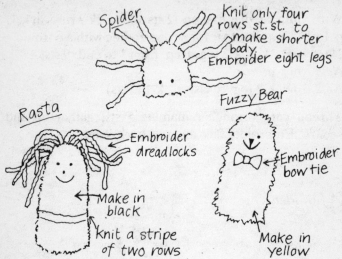

Spider — Knit only four rows st. st. to make shorter body. Embroider eight legs

Rasta — Embroider dreadlocks — Make in black — Knit a stripe of two rows

Fuzzy Bear — Embroider bow tie — Make in yellow

Using chunky and brushed chunky

With 6mm needles cast on 8 sts and work 2 rows in g.st.
Cont. in st.st. for 6 rows ending with a p. row.
Next row: *k.1, k.2 tog. Rep. from * to last 2 sts, k.2 (6 sts).
Next row: p.
Next row: k.2 tog. to end of row.
Thread yarn through remaining 3 sts, gather up and secure.

●● Egg Cosies

Egg cosies are just as easy to make as finger puppets – and as they are bigger, you can be even more inventive with your characters.

Knit one each for your mum, dad and brothers and sisters – and surprise them at the breakfast table!

Using double knitting

With 4mm needles cast on 30 sts and work 2 rows in g.st.
Cont. in st.st. for 8cm ending with a p. row.
Next row: *k.2, k.2 tog. Rep. from * to last 2 sts, k.2 (23 sts).
Next row: p.
Next row: k.2 tog. to last st., k.1 (12 sts).
Next row: p.2 tog. to end.
Thread yarn through remaining 6 sts. Embroider face, add buttons, etc., while still flat. Sew back seam.

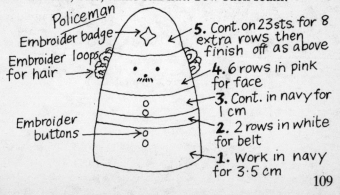

Policeman

Embroider badge →

Embroider loops for hair →

Embroider buttons →

5. Cont. on 23 sts. for 8 extra rows then finish off as above

4. 6 rows in pink for face

3. Cont. in navy for 1 cm

2. 2 rows in white for belt

1. Work in navy for 3·5 cm

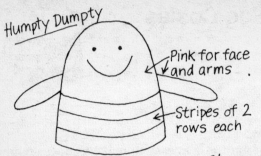

Humpty Dumpty

Pink for face and arms

Stripes of 2 rows each

Arms: cast on 2 sts. and work 2½ cm g.st.

Using mohair

With 4½ mm needles cast on 26 sts. Work 2 rows in g.st. Cont. in st.st. till work measures 8cm ending with a p. row.

Next row: *k.2, k.2 tog. Rep. from * to end (20 sts).

Next row: p.

Next row: k.2 tog. to end (10 sts).

Next row: p.2 tog. to end (5 sts).

Thread yarn through remaining 5 sts, gather up and secure. Finish as above.

Easter rabbit

Ears: fold in half lengthways

Embroider teeth in white

Easter rabbit

Make egg cosy as above in white or beige mohair. Then make ears by casting on 4 sts and working 8 rows in st.st. Fold in half lengthways and sew. Attach to egg cosy.

Using chunky and brushed chunky

With 6mm needles cast on 20 sts and work 2 rows in g.st. Cont. in st.st. until work measures 8cm ending with a p. row.

Next row: k.1, *k.2 tog., k.2. Rep. from * to last st., k.1 (15 sts).

Next row: p.

Next row: k.2 tog. to last st., k.1 (8 sts).

Next row: p.2 tog. to end (4 sts).

Thread yarn through remaining 4 sts and finish as above.

●● Snake in the Grass

A friendly snake puppet worked in stocking stitch.

You will need

2 25g balls of double knitting yarn, one in dark green **A** and one in red **B**, 2 small buttons for eyes, 1 pr 4mm needles and a wool needle.

Instructions
Face (make 2)

Using **A** cast on 24 sts and work in k.1, p.1 rib for 6.5cm.
Continue in st.st. till work measures 14cm.
Next row: k.2 tog. Knit to last 2 sts, k.2 tog.
Next row: p.
Repeat these 2 rows 5 times (12 sts).
Next row: k.2 tog. (twice). Knit to last 4 sts, k.2 tog. (twice).
Next row: p.
Cast off remaining 8 sts.

Inside mouth (make 2)

Using **B** cast on 22 sts. Work in st.st. for 4cm.
Next row: k.2 tog. Knit to last 2 sts, k.2 tog.

Next row: p.

Repeat these 2 rows 5 times (10 sts).

Next row: k.2 tog. (twice). Knit to last 4 sts, k.2 tog. (twice).

Next row: p.

Cast off remaining 6 sts.

Making up

Block all pieces and press on wrong side with a damp cloth. Take the 2 green pieces and, right sides together, sew a seam of 11cm from ribbing on both sides.

Take the two red pieces and, right sides together, sew centre seam.

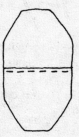

Keeping work inside out, sew inside mouth into head.

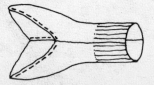

Tongue

Thread your wool needle with 1 strand of green yarn and 2 strands of red yarn, each measuring 34cm. Turn work right sides out and thread strands through centre of mouth till all six strands are level. Divide into 3 sections of 2 strands each and make a plait 9cm long.

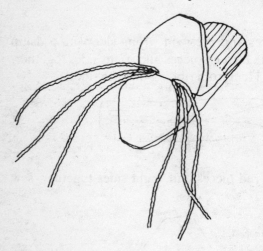

Divide into 2 sections of 3 strands each and tie. The remaining loose ends make the fork – trim level.

Finally, sew on buttons to make eyes.

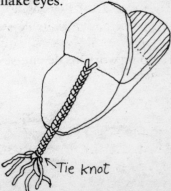

Tie knot

●● Cat in a Bag

Here is a charming present to make for a baby, for a small child, or even for a friend with a passion for cats. The bag is one straight piece of knitting, while the cat involves some simple shaping but both are worked in garter stitch.

Measurements

Cat: 10cm high
Bag: 25cm (unfolded)

You will need

1 50g ball of Talisman double knitting yarn in colour of your choice (or equivalent double-knitting yarn). Two small buttons in matching colour, 1 pr 3mm needles, cotton wool or Kapoc for stuffing and a wool needle.

Instructions
Bag

Cast on 30 sts and work in g.st. for 23 cm. To make buttonholes, k.8, y.fwd, k.2 tog. Cont. to last 9 sts, y.fwd, k.2 tog. Cont. to end. Cont. in st.st. till work measures 25cm. Cast off loosely.

Cat (make 2)

Cast on 12 sts and k.1 row.

Next row: increase 1 st. at beg. and end of row by knitting twice into first and last st.

Next row: k.

Repeat these 2 rows until you have 22 sts. Cont. on these 22 sts until work measures 4 cm.

Next row: k.2 tog. Knit to last 2 sts, k.2 tog.

Next row: k.

Rep. these two rows until you have 12 sts left.

k. 1 row

Shape head

Next row: Knit, increasing 1 st. at beg. and end of row.

Next row: k.

Rep. these 2 rows twice more (18 sts).

Cont. on these 18 sts for 2 rows.

Next row: k.2 tog. (twice). Knit to last 4 sts, k.2 tog. (twice).

Next row: k.

Cast off.

Ears (make 2)

Cast on 6 sts. K.1 row.

Next row: k.2 tog., k.2, k.2 tog. (4 sts).

Next row: k.2 tog., k.2 tog. (2 sts).

Next row: k.2 tog. Thread yarn through remaining stitch and secure.

Making up

Turn over 8cm of bag and sew side seams. Turn right side out and sew buttons in place.

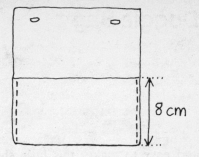

8 cm

Cat

Embroider face.

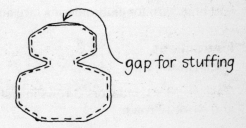

Right sides together, sew back and front together, leaving gap at top of head for stuffing. Turn right sides out and stuff sparingly with cotton wool or kapok. Sew on ears.

gap for stuffing

Put the cat in the bag and do up buttons.

●● Doggie Bag

Quick and easy to make, this little shoulder bag will make a lovely, fun present for a younger sister or brother. It is worked in stocking stitch, with 3 rows of garter stitch at the top to give a firm edge, and involves some simple shaping. The strap is made from strands of yarn plaited together.

Measurements

Approximately 13.5cm across top edge.

You will need

About 25g of Shetland quality yarn in beige or brown. (You can use synthetic yarn, but pure wool will keep its shape better.) 1 pr 4mm needles, scraps of red, brown and blue yarn for embroidering face and a wool needle.

Instructions
Face (make 2)

Cast on 28 sts and work 3 rows in g.st. Change to st.st. and work 12 rows.

Begin shaping

Next row: (right side facing) k.2 tog. Knit to last 2 sts, k.2 tog.

Next row: p.
Repeat these 2 rows 4 times (18 sts).
Next row: k.2 tog. (twice). Knit to last 4 sts, k.2 tog.
(twice).
Next row: p.
Repeat these 2 rows.
Cast off remaining 10 sts.

Making up

Lightly press both pieces with a damp cloth. Embroider
face following diagram.

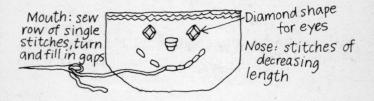

Mouth: sew row of single stitches, turn and fill in gaps

Diamond shape for eyes

Nose: stitches of decreasing length

Sew sides together leaving a gap of 2.5cm on each side,
1cm from top edge, for threading strap.

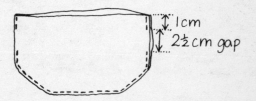

1cm
2½cm gap

Turn to right side.

Make strap

Cut 12 lengths of yarn each measuring 120cm. Put strands together and thread one end through gap on left hand side. Tie knot, leaving about 12cm free at end for ears.

Lay work on flat surface and plait till 15cm of loose ends remain. Tie through gap on right-hand side. Trim ears level.

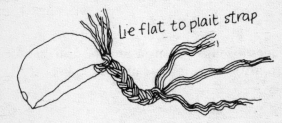

● Pocket Ted

A little teddy bear that won't take long to make – and he's just the right size to fit into your pocket.

You will need

About 25g double knitting yarn in cream, beige, brown or yellow, or colour of your choice, 1 pr 4mm needles, scraps of red, blue and brown for embroidering face, kapok or cotton wool for stuffing and a wool needle.

Instructions
Left leg

Cast on 10sts and work in g.st. for 5cm. Break off yarn and push work to end of needle.

Right leg

As above, but do not break off yarn. Slip right leg on to needle holding left leg. (You may have finished like this anyway.)

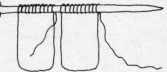

And knit across all 20 sts. Cont. in g.st. until work measures 16cm. Cast off loosely.

Arms (make 2)

Cast on 10 sts and work in g.st. for 4cm. Cast off.

Ears (make 2)

Cast on 2 sts and work 3 rows in g.st. Cast off. Darn in loose ends.

Making up

Do not press. Embroider face in top centre of work. Turn work with seam in middle of back. Sew leg seams. Sew back seam leaving a gap of 2cm, 1cm from top.

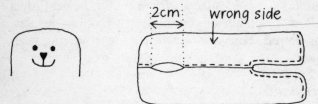

Sew arms seams, leaving gap at end:

Turn pieces right sides out. Stuff body with kapok or cotton wool and sew up gap. Stuff arms and sew one on either side of body 5cm from top of head.
Tie bow round neck. Sew on ears.

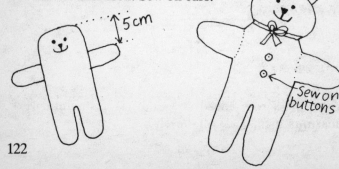

Knit for a King! . . .

(King Rollo©, of course!)

Here is a special project for more experienced knitters. There are no difficult stitches, but lots of pieces go together to make King Rollo and you will need nimble fingers for the sewing together and stuffing! But if you look at King Rollo's picture on the cover, you'll see he's well worth the effort!

The pattern we have given is based on double knitting yarn, but it would be expensive to buy separate balls of wool for each colour, so hunt around in your scrap bag and ask friends and relations if they can help. A finer quality of double knitting will work best. Because tension varies with different makes of yarn, the pattern we have given should only be used as a general guide. Use the diagram opposite to measure your pieces and use more or less stitches as needed.

Measurements

Height: 18cm

You will need

Small quantities of double knitting yarn in the following colours:

Body and arms: green and orange, or green and purple
Face and hands: pale pink
Crown: orange
Legs: light blue
Jacket: bright red and purple
Pantaloons: purple
Feet and beard: dark brown

Small quantity of black embroidery cotton for face, 1 pr 3mm needles and beans for stuffing.

Instructions

(This pattern is knitted entirely in st.st. except where rib is specified for welts and cuffs.)

Head (make 2)

Using pale pink cast on 15 sts and work in st.st. for 3½cm, ending with a p. row. Change to purple and work 4 rows.
Next row: k.2 tog. (twice). Knit to last 4 sts, k.2 tog. (twice).
Next row: p.2 tog. (twice). Pearl to last 4 sts, p. 2 tog. (twice).
Cast of remaining 7 sts.

Body (make 2)

Using green, cast on 19 sts and work in stripes of 2 rows green and 2 rows orange for 7cm, ending with a p. row. Cast off.

Legs (make 2)

Using pale blue cast on 14 sts and work in st.st. for 4 cm. Cast off.

Arms (make 2)

Using pale pink, cast on 12 sts and work in st.st. for 6 rows.
Change to green and work 5cm in stripes of 2 rows green and 2 rows orange ending with a p. row. Cast off.

Crown

Using orange, cast on 6 sts and **work 2 rows st.st. beg. with a k. row.
Next row: cast off 3 sts, k. to end.
Work 5 rows st.st.
Next row: cast on 3 sts.
Work 2 rows st.st.**
Cast off 3 sts. k. to end.
Work 5 rows st.st.
Cast on 3 sts.
Work 4 rows st.st.
Cast off 3 sts. k. to end.
Work 5 rows st.st.
Next row: cast on 3 sts.
Rep. from ** to **. Cast off.

Jerkin

Using red, cast on 42 sts and work 2 rows g.st. Change to st.st. and beg. with a k. row work 6 rows. Change to purple and work 2 rows. Change back to red and work 4 rows.
Next row: k.11, turn. Cont. in st.st. on these 11 sts for 7 rows. Cast off.
Rejoin yarn at remaining sts, k.20, turn. Cont. in st.st. on these 20 sts for 7 rows. Cast off.
Rejoin yarn at remaining 11 sts, k.11, turn. Cont. in st.st. on these 11 sts. for 7 rows. Cast off.

Pantaloons:

Left leg: using purple cast on 16 sts and work 2 rows k.1, p.1 rib.
Next row: *k.2, k. twice into next st. Rep. from * to last st., k.1 (21 sts).
Next row: p.
Cont. in st.st. for 4 rows. Break off yarn.

Right leg: as left leg, but do not break off yarn; right sides facing, slip in front of left leg.

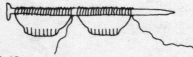

k. across all 42 sts and cont. in st.st. for 8 rows. Work 2 rows in k.1, p.1 rib. Cast off in rib.

Feet (make 2)

Using dark brown cast on 8 sts and work 12 rows. Cast off.

Making up

Darn in loose ends and press all pieces with a damp cloth. Embroider face.

Head

Right sides together, sew head seam leaving neck free.

Arms and legs

Sew seams leaving gap at ends.

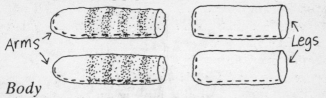

Arms → ← Legs

Body

Right sides together, sew side seams leaving gap at top *and* bottom. Turn right sides out and sew back stitch across centre.

← Back stitch through both pieces

Feet

Fold pieces in half widthwise and sew, leaving gap at top.

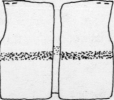

Crown

Right sides together, sew side seam.
Turn all pieces right sides out.

Jerkin

Right sides together, sew shoulder seam 1cm from each shoulder edge.

Pantaloons

Right sides together, and seam at back, sew leg seams. Sew back seam.

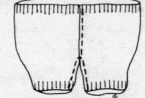

Stuffing

If you can, use small beans for stuffing. But if these are difficult to get hold of, cotton wool or kapok will do.

Stuff top of body and sew up gap. Turn and stuff bottom body and sew up gap.

Stuff arms, legs, feet and face and sew up gaps. Sew on to body, following diagram.

Embroider beard, using loops.

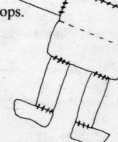

Dress him in his jacket and pantaloons. Put on his crown and you have a lovely miniature King Rollo to put in your pocket.

Read about King Rollo's adventures in David McKee's picture books, published by Andersen Press in hardback and Beaver Books in paperback. © David McKee.